EVERYTHING ELSE
IN THE WORLD

EVERYTHING ELSE
IN THE WORLD

poems

Stephen Dunn

W. W. Norton & Company   New York   London

For information about permission to reproduce selections from this book,
write to Permissions, W. W. Norton & Company, Inc., 500 Fifth Avenue,
New York, NY 10110

Manufacturing by The Courier Companies, Inc.

Book design by Anna Oler

Library of Congress Cataloging-in-Publication Data

Dunn, Stephen, date.
Everything else in the world : poems / Stephen Dunn.— 1st ed.
p. cm.
ISBN-13: 978-0-393-06239-7 (hardcover)
ISBN-10: 0-393-06239-2 (hardcover)
I. Title.
PS3554.U49E84 2006
811'.54—dc22

2006003697

ISBN 978-0-393-33038-0 pbk.

W. W. Norton & Company, Inc.
500 Fifth Avenue, New York, N.Y. 10110
www.wwnorton.com

W. W. Norton & Company Ltd.
Castle House, 75/76 Wells Street, London W1T 3QT

2 3 4 5 6 7 8 9 0

for Kenny & Ann

CONTENTS

ACKNOWLEDGMENTS

The following poems have appeared or will appear in these journals:

AGNI: "My Ghost," "The Soul's Agents"

The American Poetry Review: "Everything Else in the World," "Summer Nocturne," "What I Might Say if I Could," "You'd Be Right"

Bat City Review: "How to Write a Dream Poem"

Free Lunch: "Replicas"

The Georgia Review: "The Kiss," "The Telling of Grandmother's Secret," "The Land of Is"

The Gettysburg Review: "The Lost Thing," "I Caught Myself Thinking the Horizon," "Time"

The Iowa Review: "No Wonder," "Process," "Where He Found Himself," "Postcard from Tortola"

LIT: "*Madrugada*," "A Small Part"

Mid-American Review: "Poker Night in Tornado Alley"

New England Review: "Lucky," "Inventing Wallace Stevens"

Nightsun: "Returning to the Ravens"

Poetry: "From the Tower at the Top of the Winding Stairs," "Salvation"

Praire Schooner: "Bad Plants," "The Slow Surge," "Emptiness," "At His House," "Cardinal Cardinal," "Explanations"

32 Poems: "Cut and Break"

Xconnect: "Signs"

The Yale Review: "The Unrecorded Conversation"

Many thanks to Barbara Hurd, Jill Rosser, and Sam Toperoff—my indispensable readers, and especially to Lawrence Raab for his great scrupulousness. And to my editor Carol Houck Smith, whose significance is lauded in "Signs," which is dedicated to her.

"To be of more than one heart."

—Victoria Hearne

"Eve ate to break the monotony. Eve ate to enjoy the appetite it would give her."

—William Gass

ONE

A SMALL PART

The summer I discovered my heart
is at best an instrument of approximation
and the mind is asked to ratify
every blood rush sent its way

was the same summer I stared
at the slate gray sea well beyond dusk,
learning how exquisitely
I could feel sorry for myself.

It was personal—the receding tide,
the absent, arbitrary wind.
I had a small part in the great comedy,
and hardly knew it. No excuse,

but I was so young I believed
Ayn Rand had a handle on truth—
secular, heroically severe. Be a man
of unwavering principle, I told others,

and what happens to the poor
is entirely their fault. No wonder
that girl left me in August, a stillness
in the air. I was one of those lunatics

of a single idea, or maybe even worse—
I kissed wrong, or wasn't brave enough
to admit I was confused.
Many summers later I'd learn to love

the shadows illumination creates.
But experience always occurs too late
to undo what's been done. The hint
of moon above an unperturbable sea,

and that young man, that poor me,
staring ahead—everything is as it was.
And of course has been changed.
I got over it. I've never been the same.

THE LOST THING

The truth is
it never belonged to anybody.
It's not a music box or locket;
it doesn't bear our initials.
It has none of the tragic glamour
of a lost child, won't be found
on any front page. It's like
the river that confuses
search dogs, like the promise
on the far side of the ellipsis.
Look for it in the margins,
is the conventional wisdom.
Look for it as late afternoon light
dips below the horizon.
But it's not to be seen.
Nor does it have a heart
or give off any signal.
It's as if . . . is how some of us
keep trying to reach it.
Once, long ago, I felt sure
I was in its vicinity.

LUCKY

> Loyal obedience to the rules jointly defined
> and freely accepted.
> —Albert Camus, on why his true lessons
> in morality came from sports

Lucky that we didn't know the games we played
  were teaching us about boundaries
and integrity; it would have smacked of school,

we who longed for recess. And lucky—when exiled
  to right field, or not chosen at all—
we didn't know the lesson was injustice,

just how much of it we could tolerate.
  But always there'd be the boys
who never got it, calling foul when foul

there wasn't, marking with an X the spot
  where the ball didn't hit.
Where are they now? What are they doing?

Lucky that some of us who loved recess
  came to love school,
found the books that gave us a few words

for what the aggrieved already knew. Lucky
   that within rules
freely accepted we came to recognize a heart

can be ferocious, a mind devious and fair.

SALVATION

Finally, I gave up on obeisance,
and refused to welcome
either retribution or the tease

of sunny days. As for the can't-be-
seen, the sum-of-all-details,
the One—oh when it came

to salvation I was only sure
I needed to be spared
someone else's version of it.

The small prayers I devised
had in them the hard sounds
of *split* and *frost*.

In the beaconless dark
I wanted them to speak
as if it made sense to speak

to what isn't there.
I wanted them to startle
by how little they asked.

MY GHOST

The desirable place is always another place,
my father said. The restlessness continues.
His voice was calm, though disembodied.
He didn't appear to be complaining.
And it doesn't matter, he added.

Even at that moment I knew I was speaking
to myself. You were dreaming, my wife said,
and I told her the half of it
that tries to masquerade as all—his exact words,
no mention of his face being mine.

It was clear from her smile
she was translating those words,
clearer still when she asked
a little too politely
if I'd please take out the dog.

But of course ours is a desirable place,
I was tempted to insist, or, How lucky,
my dear, that we're restless together.
I said neither, didn't want to feel
I had to just then. Maybe later.

An outgoing man, my father once held back
a truth that could have rescued him from sadness.
Now he roams the night, my inheritance
in every word I hear him speak. He vanishes,
returns, no place for him in this entire world.

WHAT I MIGHT SAY IF I COULD

You're a Hutu with a machete, a Serb with orders,
you're one more body in a grave they made you dig.
Or, almost worse, you're alive to tell the story,
the most silent man on earth.

Here, rhododendrons are blooming, and cicadas
are waking from their long sleep.
I need not tell you how fast a good country
can become a hateful, hated thing.

Born in the wrong place at the wrong time
to parents wronged by their parents
and ruled by some crazed utopian with a plan—
no ice-cream cone for you, no summer at the shore.

I know you can't believe suffering leads to anything
but more suffering, or that wisdom waits
in some survivor's room at the end of a hall.
What good to tell you that sometimes it does?

Sometimes has the future in it, and wisdom,
you must fear, is what victors think is theirs.
You can't even be sure of a full bowl
of rice, and you've forgotten how to sing.

Clouds with periods of sun, says our weatherman.
Unlike some of us, he never intends to lie.
Many here who look no further than their yards
believe God has a design.

EMPTINESS

I've learned mine can't be filled,
only alchemized. Many times
it's become a paragraph or a page.
But usually I've hidden it,
not knowing until too late
how enormous it grows in its dark.
Or how obvious it gets
when I've donned, say, my good
cordovans and my fine tweed vest
and walked into a room with a smile.
I might as well have been a man
with a fez and a faux silver cane.

Better, I know now, to dress it plain,
to say out loud
to some right person
in some right place
that there's something not there
in me, something I can't name.
That some right person
has just lit a fire under the kettle.
She hasn't said a word.
Beneath her blue shawl
she, too, conceals a world.

But she's been amazed
how much I seem to need my emptiness,
amazed I won't let it go.

WHERE HE FOUND HIMSELF

The new man unfolded a map and pointed
to a dark spot on it. "See, that's how
far away I feel all the time, right here,
among all of you," he said.
    "Yes," John the gentle mule replied,
"alienation is clearly your happiness."
But the group leader interrupted,
"Now, now, let's hear him out,
let's try to be fair." The new man felt
the familiar comfort of everyone against him.

    He went on about the stupidities
of love, life itself as one long foreclosure,
until another man said, "I was a hog,
a terrible hog, and now I'm a llama."
To which another added, "And me, I was a wolf.
Now children walk up to me, unafraid."

    The group leader asked the new man,
"What kind of animal have you been?"
"A rat that wants to remain a rat," he said,
and the group began to soften
as they remembered their own early days,
the pain before the transformation.

THE UNRECORDED CONVERSATION

> Isolation is the indispensable component
> of human happiness.   —Glenn Gould

Maybe genius is its own nourishment,
I wouldn't know.
Gould didn't need much more than Bach
whom he devoured
and so beautifully gave back
we forgave him his withdrawal from us.
Food frightened him, as people did,
though it was known he loved
to call Barbra Streisand at 3 a.m.
He must have liked hearing in her voice
the presence of sleep, the slightest variation.

Jeanne Moreau was in her late sixties
when I heard her say she lived alone,
adding, *by choice*—a smile in her words
missed by the interviewer who pushed
ahead, pleased to let us hear a woman
who'd learned to live *sans* men. "What
do you like best about your solitude?"
asked the interviewer. "Ah," Moreau said,
"inviting people into it," and I was Jules
or maybe Jim and in love again.

Gould retreated to his studio
at thirty-one, keeping his distance
from microphones and their germs.
He needed to control sound, edit out
imperfection. His were the only hands
that touched the keys, turned the dials.

In my dream, Moreau calls, inviting him in.
It's easy for Gould to refuse,
which he does in French,
one of his languages, and with charm,
one of the vestiges of the life
he can no longer bear to live.

TIME

I stood still, feeling it move by.
If only I could begin
to have a good time, I said

to myself, I could elongate
the present by the eternity
of a second or two. I'd done it before.

Kiss me, I said to the universe,
because it's through play
that we impede the slavish tock

from following the inexorable tick.
Unbutton my shirt, I implored.
But the universe wasn't in the mood.

Time seemed to hesitate, that's all.
The future was waiting for it
with open mouth and no regrets,

and time was as weak as any of us.
Meanwhile the past was feeling
unremembered, afraid it might cease

to exist. If only I could begin to have
a good time, I said to the past,
I'd remember you always.

But by then I was speaking
to the most recent past, the milk
of the present still on its lips.

REPLICAS

When it became clear aliens were working here
with their dead-giveaway, perfectly cut Armani suits,
excessive politeness, and those ray guns
disguised as cell phones tucked into their belts,
I decided we had two choices: cocktail party
to befriend them, or massive air strikes (I joked
at the Board meeting) on what might be a hospital
for children with rare diseases, but could
as easily be where these aliens spawned and lived.
Cocktail party it was, and they came
with their gorgeous women dressed like replicas
of gorgeous women, and though they sipped
their martinis as if they'd graduated
from some finishing school between their world
and ours, I must admit they were good company,
talking ball scores and GNP, even movies,
and how bright and inviting the stars seemed
from my porch. I found myself almost
having sympathy for what certain people will do
to fit in, until I remembered they might want
to take over, maybe even blow things up.
And when the dog barked from the other room,
the way she does when some creature is nearby,
about to cross an invisible line, I was sure

I couldn't afford to trust appearances ever again.
Then it was time to leave, and they left,
saying at the door what a good evening they'd had.
Each of them used the same words,
like people who've been trained in sales,
and as they moved to their Miatas and Audis
I noted the bare shoulders of their women
were the barest shoulders I'd ever seen,
as if they needed only the night as a shawl.

THE SOUL'S AGENTS

Every night before bed, say for a week,
we recommend admitting a lie
or a deception, sotto voce, a rogue's prayer
to the soul you know you have,
no matter how tattered or dormant.
Trust us, your secrets differentiate you
from no one, but the soul awakens
a little when it hears them.
We have its interests at heart,
which means your interests as well.

Try to practice unsettling
what remains settled in you—
those ideas, for example,
inherited, still untested.
And if only you could raise
your hypocrisy to the level of art,
like forgery, there might be
real hope for you.

Some people of course expect
to be rewarded for stumbling
and rising from the floor
and stumbling again, but we give

no credit for living. We favor vitality
over goodness, even over effort;
we love a great belly laugh
more than anything.

In your case we do worry
there may not be enough
quarrel in you, or enough courage
to acknowledge your worst inclinations.
Know that the soul converts them
into tenderness. Nothing pleases it more.

So next week why not admit
that what Raskolnikov did
has always made you dream?
The more you expose yourself
the more you become unrecognizable.
Remember, we are here to help.
What you decide to keep
from the world, tell us. We understand
everything. We pass it on.

YOU'D BE RIGHT

He often needed two women. Just one—
how unfair to expect from her so much!
Intelligence before and after sex,
a certain naughtiness during,
gifts of companionship and solitude.
But he liked the day-to-day of marriage
and its important unimportances,
quiet moments made livable
by the occasional promise of a fiesta.
And though he knew he wasn't enough
for her either, and always assumed
she had similar thoughts, if not secrets,
nevertheless you may be thinking cad,

maybe even monster, you who've been happy,
or differently unhappy, or obeyed all your life
some good rule. And you'd be right
if you guessed his wife's eventual coolness,
her turning away, and, when he didn't leave,
the slow rise of the other woman's disappointment,
which would turn to anger, then to sadness.
You'd be right, but can you imagine what joys
accrue to the needy over a lifetime of seeking love?
Can you say you're not envious, or that you're sure
it wasn't worth what he risked and lost?

EVERYTHING ELSE IN THE WORLD

Too young to take pleasure
from those privileged glimpses
we're sometimes given after failure,
or to see the hidden opportunity
in not getting what we want,
each day I subwayed into Manhattan

in my new, blue serge suit,
looking for work. College, I thought,
had whitened my collar, set me up,
but I'd majored in history.
What did I know about the world?

At interviews, if asked about the world,
I might have responded—citing Carlyle—
Great men make it go, I want to be one of those.
But they wanted someone entry-level,
pleased for a while to be small.

Others got the jobs;
no doubt, later in the day, the girls.
At Horn & Hardarts, for solace
at lunchtime, I'd make a sandwich emerge
from its cell of pristine glass.
It took just a nickel and a dime.

Nickels and dimes could make
a middleman disappear, easy as that,
no big deal, a life or two
destroyed, others improved.
But I wasn't afraid of capitalism.
All I wanted was a job like a book
so good I'd be finishing it
for the rest of my life.

Had my education failed me?
I felt a hankering for the sublime,
its dangerous subversions
of the daily grind.
Oh I took a dull, well-paying job.
History major? the interviewer said, I think
you might be good at designing brochures.

I was. Which filled me with desire
for almost everything else in the world.

TWO

THE LAND OF IS

The woman whose backpack I helped lift
to the baggage rack in that suddenly sweet
compartment of a train was an art historian
from Marseilles. We talked Giotto
all the way to Naples, and fell asleep
in each other's arms.

Or was this an episode partially lived,
partially dreamed?

After my old Ford broke down in Yellowstone,
those grizzlies I invented, especially the one
standing upright near her cubs
as if declaring *no pasarán*—that story
has just the right feel.
Trust me. Even the Spanish belongs.

With that bar fight in Elko, however,
there's much still to solve. Should he be Mexican
because he was Mexican? And when,
exactly, should he pull his knife?
I keep changing my mind, sure only
of the scar on my arm—the importance
of mentioning it, I mean.

It's clear that a story not tilted
will rarely stand up. But sometimes

I find myself in the land of is, helpless
before the tyranny of this
or that sufficient thing.
That large wooden horse, for example,
with car parts for a head—the one
that silhouettes my property's edge—

I admit I placed it there, and love at dusk
to see the blackbirds ride its back
and the field of barley it overlooks
turn dark purple as night descends.

Strange horse, it is what it is,
all funk and fact, in a beautiful spot.
What could be worse?
I can't muster the slightest impulse
to make it rear up, or run amok.

POSTCARD FROM TORTOLA

I've never been to Tortola,
though many times I've drifted
to the vast principality of elsewhere
where, no doubt, a Tortola must be,
so I can attest the weather is the weather
I've brought with me, overcast
with periods of sun, always a low
following a high, and the natives
impoverished and gay. You wouldn't
like it here. Go elsewhere. One person's
Tortola is another's Sadness-by-the-Sea.
The duty from which you're absolved
in the duty-free shops comes with a price.
On the other hand, it's beautiful—
the water turquoise, the breeze a constant
caress. Some people actually love
that there's singing in the streets.

RETURNING TO THE RAVENS

For Madeleine & Joel

Loudly announcing arrivals and departures,
the ravens in Ketchikan—
those crows on steroids—ruled the cedars
outside my hotel window.
Built only for short flights, they soon
worked the street, full of posture and strut,
big-chested silly guys, some mischief afoot.
Then there were the eagles, fierce
and humorless, as the efficient often are,
up there at such a distance
their reputation could never diminish.
I felt I was watching privilege,
the advantages of birth, and would return
each day to where the ravens gathered,
happy to see their I've-got-a-secret smirks.
No doubt it was time to go home,
let the birds be birds, without choice.
The morning I left, raucous gulls circled
white fishing boats in the harbor.
Democrats of a catch not theirs,
they made no distinction between leftovers
and meals achieved by headlong dives

and perfect, clean entries. All appetite,
they just wanted what they wanted.
A light rain was falling, everything gray.
Among plenitude, the gulls squabbled,
the sky undulant with their trashy beauty.

MADRUGADA

No word for it in English, that time
between midnight and dawn. Most of us
are asleep by then, outrunning leopards
on blue lawns, or avenging our daily lives.
But in South America many are awake.
I see them dancing in the *madrugada*
all *madrugada* long. Even those working
quietly in their rooms at 3 a.m.—
it pleases me to think—are doing so
in the *madrugada*. I love how life nags
and language responds.
But if I were to fly to Caracas or Lima
to live the word and to say it out loud,
no doubt it would start to rhyme
with grunts from bar fights
and the muffled cries of women
forced into cars, and in dim-lit rooms
the silence of money sliding
into someone's hand. *Madrugada,*
I might say then, without pleasure,
its meaning so consonant with the world.

INVENTING WALLACE STEVENS

You'll need a certain amount of fertile American soil
and a bunch of paysans. You'll need the ever-hooded
sea and a woman a man could hide behind
while singing there—a sleight-of-hand man
who once, say, was a small time roller of big cigars.
You'll have to put them all in a large body, dress it
in a business suit and tie, and send it off to the office,
not allowing it to wink at widows while on the job.
On the walk home, though, block by block,
imagine things going round and again going round
in his head, until Hartford is becoming Pascagoula,
his briefcase a guitar. Then those complacencies
when he opens the door, how downward to darkness
things seem for him at dinner. It's important,
as counterpoint, to register his wife's sadness
after asking him about indemnities, and his day.
The silences. How often he must have been
in some wilderness in Tennessee. Get him to his room
as soon as you can. Red weather and some wild
tunk-a-tunk sublime await him there, but he'll need
quieter music, too, perhaps an oboe gracing a clavier
if things rightly are to occur as they occur.

CRITICS

Listen to their voices, that's all right,
but do not strain to hear your name.
Their job sometimes is to winnow
and omit. Yours is to go on.

Make believe you're watching yourself
walk back to a limousine
like a character in a film
seen from a distance.
Someone awaits you there,

but you are now someone else,
free to veer
into wild, unmown fields
or housing developments—
traces of blood, perhaps,
on the poorly lit stairs.

No matter what their voices say,
you'll want to ready yourself
to open a different kind of door.

But repeat yourself if you want.
Remember the sky can be magnificent
day after day, and the mailman is loved
who braves the storm.

Sometimes you'll hear their voices
lilt, trip into praise.
It will be hard not to listen for your name.

Your job is to show up, continue on.

PROCESS

I feel nothing and nothing's in my head,
but something's about to happen
that happens to certain trees in seedtime.
Along come some birds and the wind
(bearing with them those *n* and *d* sounds)
and suddenly I'm on my way—

though I'm still in my room—
to a clearing in the woods, beyond which
lies a city and its words—
skyscraper, midnight jazz, traffic jam—
words I like the texture of
that remind me of her and that moment. . . .

So now my heart is dangerously full,
I know too well where I'm going—
I'm on the verge of becoming
one of the dullest men on earth.
Time to introduce something foreign
to impede the easy
arrival, the metronomic hum

of business as usual. But just as likely
I'm stuck in that field where I started.
The ground is hard
and my tools seem old and nothing
reminds me of nothing. I move
a little surface dirt around, that's all.

Still, there's an opening I can't yet see,
history says so, and in it, perhaps,
acrobats will abandon a circus,
office workers break into arias—
all because of that evening
she walked into the bar at the Blue Note
to get out of the pouring rain.

HOW TO WRITE A DREAM POEM

Do not try to be faithful.
Change the tunnel to a mountain road
in a South American country, Bolivia
if you need those sounds,
otherwise Chile is a place where
something unfortunate might happen
to someone like you.
Try to avoid elevators descending
at terrible speeds, and though
your predicament should occur
in the evening, do not use dark
except to suggest the complexion
of that young boy
who will report you missing.
A light rain, if you need atmospherics at all.
No thunderstorms, no fallen trees.
So you're on a mountain road
in Chile and you're lost.
Two men wearing fatigues in a jeep
ask you about the weather in heaven,
and you start to run
but you're standing still, and one of them,
the big one with the mustache and the scar,
hands you what seems like a lily,

freshly cut. Take it, he says, it's yours,
and take this pigeon too, your happiness
is ours. Then they drive away.
It will be important around now
not to mention Bosch or Magritte,
though it will be a good time to wonder
out loud what your dream is about.
Allow yourself to be wrong.
Your readers need to have ideas
of their own, and they will be impatient
with you anyway. Why should we care?
they'll be thinking. What does this
have to do with us?
The large animal that appears out of
the Chilean shadows has someone else
in mind. That blood trail shouldn't be yours.
Jump-cut, perhaps to a tavern
where there's an illusion of safety.
When a toothless woman promises
for a mere kiss that she'll be your guide,
refuse her. She might be
that large animal. Yes, hint that she is.
In dreams shape-shifting is as normal
as fabulous acts of revenge.

But everything in your poem
should depend on arrangement
more than statement, on enchantment
more than any specific, disabling fear.
And when it comes time for you to wake,
no alarm, please. Have the light,
as it does, slowly make you conscious
that it's morning and you're alive.
No problem with being disturbed for a while.
Such things linger. But go down
to breakfast and take your readers with you.
Remember, they're in a world
that's provisional, and yours.
Make some coffee for them. Tell them
the melons are in season, and perfectly chilled.

SIGNS

For Carol Houck Smith

Earlier, a slow child in the vicinity
of a Slow Children sign, a boy
just taking his time, his book bag
weighing him down, and now—
driving past Caution: Falling
Rock Zone—an actual fallen rock
right in the middle of the Interstate!
I call 911, report it—the danger—
one loose rock suggesting many,
some hilltop family of them
finally about to become unglued.

I say the signs have started to come true,
and laugh, but the operator is serious,
only wants to know where, and who.
I give her the hard facts, the everything
she wants. I'm a good citizen today.
Soon I'll even stop at Stop,

then at red stop again, always careful
about my braveries. Only late at night,
nobody around, have I gunned it,

gone right on through, felt the outlaw
in me stir, smiled that inward smile.

Truth is, I'd be happy in this world
to be quietly significant
like a good editor.
I'd like to improve Slow Children,
for example, by putting in
that comma where it belongs.

I'm almost home. The increase in Jesus
bumper stickers has been telling me so.
At Finzel near Little Savage in big letters
at the end of a driveway: Beware Dog,
and there he is, the Beware Dog
halfway between the house and the road,
sleeping or waiting, I'll never know.

MOONRAKERS

Moonrakers were men of the English county
of Wiltshire caught raking a pond for kegs
of smuggled brandy, who feigned madness
to fool the revenue men by saying
they were raking out the moon.

We rippled the moon for them,
the government men. We pretended to be sad
when it slid through our fingers
and shape-shifted back into itself.
We offered them a cup of moon
after we drank a cup ourselves
so they'd think us mad and leave us
alone with what we'd hidden.

They retreated, we suspected not for long.
We knew they didn't believe us—
couldn't hide their government posture
or what government work does to a heart.
Earnest, stolid, impersonating trees,
they were watching, we were sure,
from what they thought to be their blind.

We took out our fiddles and fiddled
as if moon-driven, sang as if daft.
We did it because that's what we did
when there seemed nothing left to do.
But in the doing we made music
that felt necessary and ours, and after
we escaped in the ever-darkening dark
we played it for the rest of our lives.

THE TELLING OF
GRANDMOTHER'S SECRET

"Belle's story was that she came over from
Prince Edward Island to Boston when she was
sixteen to be a nurse's apprentice, but that wasn't
exactly true. She got pregnant, had the child—
oh it's a long story. The truth is she was sent
away in shame." —Aunt Jessica, age 87

Trying to desire nothing,
I walked up Gravel Hill Drive,
then back, the day after Jessica's call.
But my disquiet wouldn't be quieted.
I was clear proof that unless you sat
very still, did the necessary work,
Zen was just a name, a kind of flirtation.

Still, nice to know there was a religion you could fail
without worrying about eternal damnation,
a conundrum troubling you instead of a precept.

Nice also to ramble toward your subject,
sensing nobody cares about it but you,
feeling those first narrative latitudes,
the narrowings as you go. Already the secret

had visited my sleep, sat down with me
at breakfast, rubbing the dark from its eyes.
What confidence it had. Imagine,
this suddenly unlocked thing
believing it was irresistible as is.

     "I'm the only one left who knows,"
Jessica explained, then couldn't stop herself.
With each call the secret grew larger,
and I'd carry it out into the vagaries
of late October—one morning a clear view
of Savage Mountain, the next a cold mist—
aware that every story needed atmosphere
in order to exist.

     And then the surprise of atmosphere
in collusion with memory, grandmother's silence
coming back to me, and her kindness, for the first time,
feeling like an achievement. There she was,
cooking our meals, running the house,
my ill mother barely able to assist.
And there was her secret, pressing in
on her and down, asking for release.

That she was impregnated by her teacher at age fifteen,
that the teacher married her and on the wedding night
disappeared forever, that she gave the baby to a relative
to raise, that she'd been sent away—not over—
to America, where she converted shame into silence,
married again, becoming a bigamist, that her husband
and daughter and my brother and I never knew,

all this speaks to the awkwardness of exposition
and of a concealment so gifted
it's impossible to know the degree
to which it also was tragic—a life denied,
a child left behind. As family secrets go,

nothing for the tabloids, no one
beaten senseless, or murdered in bed.
But for me things to walk off, and toward,

about which two dogs from the house
atop Gravel Hill had something to say.
Protective of what they hardly understood,
they charged, barked—good dogs, really,
their tails giving them away, and I turned,
started back, the secret seeming less and less

mine, part landscape now,
part the words used in its behalf.

A man in a pickup drove by,
his two raised fingers signaling, what?
That unlikely comrades were possible
in this world? That we share a code?
But he'd come so suspiciously
out of the narrative blue.

If you meet the Buddha on the road,
kill him, Buddhists say, worried
about anyone bearing indispensable news.

Lucky for that man he didn't stop,
I might have had to eliminate him.
Instead, something grandmotherly—
it must have been grandmotherly—
insisted I just let him be a man
making his way home.
Open a door for him, said that something,
now close it so he's safe within.

I descended the hill,
the dogs still yapping as if certain
they were the cause. Up ahead,
the sudden sun through the trees
had speckled my driveway,
and, at its end, where gravel gives way
to macadam, there was the circle

          that allows things
to be dropped off at the front door.
It was all shadowy and clear,
and moving toward it I felt
the odd, muted pleasure that comes
when you realize you've only just begun
to know how you feel.

THREE

INFATUATION

Let's just say
she was like the long absent sun
that calls us out of our houses
and into a promise
that suddenly feels so welcome
we're as helpless
as any crocus or daffodil.

Yet I was no dumb flower.
All morning I wondered
how I might resist
a feeling like this.
A part of me wanted to take
the February snow
and the February emptiness

and make a plan so stoical,
so clear-eyed,
my heart might pause
a moment, become for once
the mind's thing.

But there she was—at my door.
Let's go somewhere, she said,
and it didn't matter that the wind
had come up or that the cold
we were about to walk into
was certain to sting and burn.

THE KISS

> She pressed her lips to mind.
>
> —a typo

How many years I must have yearned
for someone's lips against mind.
Pheromones, newly born, were floating
between us. There was hardly any air.

She kissed me again, reaching that place
that sends messages to toes and fingertips,
then all the way to something like home.
Some music was playing on its own.

Nothing like a woman who knows
to kiss the right thing at the right time,
then kisses the things she's missed.
How had I ever settled for less?

I was thinking this is intelligence,
this is the wisest tongue
since the Oracle got into a Greek's ear,
speaking sense. It's the Good,

defining itself. I was out of my mind.
She was in. We married as soon as we could.

SUMMER NOCTURNE

> Let us love this distance, since those
> who do not love each other are
> not separated.   —Simone Weil

Night without you, and the dog barking at the silence,
no doubt at what's *in* the silence,
a deer perhaps pruning the rhododendron
or that raccoon with its brilliant fingers
testing the garbage can lid by the shed.

Night I've chosen a book to help me think
about the long that's in longing, "the space across
which desire reaches." Night that finally needs music
to quiet the dog and whatever enormous animal
night itself is, appetite without limit.

Since I seem to want to be hurt a little,
it's Stan Getz and "It Never Entered My Mind,"
and to back him up Johnnie Walker Black
coming down now from the cabinet to sing
of its twelve lonely years in the dark.

Night of small revelations, night of odd comfort.
Starting to love this distance.
Starting to feel how present you are in it.

BAD PLANTS

Driven to take over by imperatives beyond their control,
it takes more than good reasons
to stop them—kudzu and crown vetch, for example,
villains that even sound villainous.

Sometimes they're called invasive species, sometimes—
and this is my preference—exotics,
which suggests the beautiful and the dangerous
in one package,

like purple loosestrife, and often life as I've known it.
I'm not surprised that many
have beautiful names, like thistle or honeysuckle.
Even the well-thought-of violet

tends to muscle in, shove aside. All of them are inclined
to choke out what's native.
Bad plants? Nature of course would say, Careful now,
watch your language, let's just see

what survives. But I've been bad enough myself
to know it can be dangerous
to allow the natural to be natural. Never make a deal,
I'd say, with kudzu,

or become purple loosestrife's Neville Chamberlain.
And let's not praise plants either
which tend to keep to themselves, be good citizens.
No rewards

for being what only you can be. Sure, though,
pick a violet
for your best girl. Pick several. Let love when it can
be a form of containment.

THE SLOW SURGE

How sweetly disappeared the silky distraction
of her clothes, and before that the delicacy
with which she stepped out of her shoes.

Can one ever unlearn what one knows?
In postcoital calm I was at home
in the great, minor world

of flesh, languor, and whispery talk.
Soon, I knew, the slow surge of dawn
would give way to rush hour and chores.

It would be hard to ignore the ugliness—
the already brutal century,
the cold, spireless malls—everything the mind

lets in after lovemaking has run its course,
when even a breast that excited you so
is merely companionable, a place to rest your hand.

AT HIS HOUSE

In my friend's face it's not easy to separate
what's serenity, what's despair.
What the mouth suggests the eyes correct,

and what looks like acceptance
is a kind of détente, the world allowed
to encroach only so far.

At his house, we put aside
the large questions: Is there? And if so?
replace them with simple chores.

We bring vegetables in from the garden.
We shuck corn. Is it possible
to be a good citizen without saying a word?

Both his wives thought not, wanted love
to have a language he never learned.
He'd make wine for them from dandelions.

Sundays he'd serve them breakfast in bed.
In his toolbox he was sure he had a tool
for whatever needed to be fixed.

The deed reveals the man, he says.
I don't tell him that it's behind deeds
he and I often hide.

I've got a face for noon, a face for dusk,
a fact he lets slide. Both of us think friendship
is about what needn't be said.

It seems we're a couple of halves, men
almost here, hardly there. At his house less
feels good. I always come back for more.

CARDINAL CARDINAL

You're a male attacking the window
where your rival appears, dangerous
and familiar. You know exactly
what that bird has in mind.
Important, therefore, to defeat it

but you have a brain no bigger
than your enemy's. The odds
are against you, as they were
when the female was given all that
quiet beauty. You're bright red,

as is the bird you attack, and anyone
who's ever been loud and horny
understands the problem. Nothing
is likely to happen if you go on like this
unless suddenly you're frightened into sense,

which is exactly what occurs, but by then
your beak is sore, and your friends
are formulating an owl decal joke
at your expense, the owl decal on the window
that has sent you back to the trees

where you have to please the subtle
brown thing with qualities you're not sure
you have. Tell us about the ceremony—
the seed you bring to her like a kiss,
the delicacy with which she accepts it.

I CAUGHT MYSELF THINKING
THE HORIZON

I caught myself thinking the horizon
is nothing more than a flat screen of sky,
as if I were looking for a reason to stay
in my house, to dare not, seek not, don't.

That night, in the lawlessness of sleep,
riding a palomino
on a vast, grassy expanse,
I tried to escape a band of gauchos.

"I'm not sorry," I turned to tell them.
"Trespasser!" they hollered,
which somehow made me happy,
though their lassos circled near,

which was when my wife touched me
awake, said that I'd said out loud
something about the sanctuary of a river
and a horse too exhausted to get me there.

Next day I was back, of course,
where I started, on pause, watching
from my window a few wispy clouds
at the mercy of the wind.

What hard work adventure is, I thought,
even in dreams. There again was the horizon,
always about to vanish. All I had to do
was walk in its direction.

POKER NIGHT IN TORNADO ALLEY

Two blasts of the town siren was a warning,
    a maybe.
Three—the real thing had been sighted.

But at my friend Al's farmhouse, as the dark
    clouds gathered,
the game was so good we couldn't stop playing.

It was Minnesota, the prairie, and the warnings
    seemed to add something
to our low stakes, and the hard lives of men

who, earlier, had dismounted Caterpillars
    and John Deeres,
left the flat, loamy fields behind them.

I was the bad influence from New York,
    raiser of the ante,
introducer of Hold 'Em. It was my fault,

Al's wife said later, that her husband was bluffing
    when he should have been running.
Nor could she resist pointing out it was stud

we were playing, seven card, when that siren
    blasted thrice
and we finally hurried to our obedient cars.

The wisdom was go north, and north we went,
    suddenly silent, the radio telling us
the approximate drift of that swirling thing

we'd gambled with. When it seemed safe
    we turned back to find
Al's barn was gone, hardly a trace of it,

but his house was intact, and all the chips
    in their sweet, neat stacks.
I called my wife to tell her everything,

or, as husbands do, some of everything.
    Al's opening the beer, I said,
I'm all right, and, no, I'll still be home late.

NO WONDER

We were sitting in our Adirondacks
high up in the Appalachians,
sipping margaritas. Our dog Bigdog
chewed spikes of grass, worried perhaps
we'd again get out the suitcase,
and time immeasurable and those nights
with strangers would commence.
But we were staying put. The clouds
had moved on, multiplying
the stars. Though we missed
the penumbra around the moon
and its curious shadows, not to mention
the feeling that we might be concealed,
we welcomed the suddenly omnipresent
sky, toasted it with those margaritas.
No wonder so many before us—
before electricity, before science
and its more verifiable maybes—
dreamed an existence up there.
They didn't have suitcases to pack.
They weren't lucky like us
to have an animal they didn't need
to eat. Hear that, Bigdog? I said,

your worries should have a little more
historical perspective. This world
is ours. We're going nowhere tonight.

CUT AND BREAK

Each morning the sullen but excellent masons
arrived at six to cut and lay stone
for the rising walls of our walkway.
Hung over, they worked deliberately, didn't care
that anyone might be sleeping or disturbed.
We learned not to speak to them before noon.

It was western Maryland; for me a new home,
new love, at once connected and removed.
Guns and Jesus rhymed on many a pickup.
The local newspaper ransacked
the Bible to edify and guide. Democracy:
how hard to like it every hour of the day.

Meanwhile, when the stonemasons spoke
they cursed. When they were silent
they were making noise. At 6 a.m. I could think
of a few freedoms I wished to curtail.
But of course they worked with what wouldn't
easily yield. They had to cut and break

before they could make anything whole.
I should have been all sympathy,
I who'd recently torn apart a marriage,

discovered what was and wasn't there.
In a few weeks the walkway was finished.
They were out of my life, gone.

Something solid remained, and the mountains
seemed to collect around us,
seemed even to redefine the sky,
but not for long. In this foreignness
I recognized an elsewhere
I carried with me, no one's fault.

Yet my love had a way of finding me
wherever I was. And soon I'd meet a man
whose decline in tennis matched mine,
and another I knew would be a friend
after I saw the stunning useless art he made
out of metal, discarded things.

EXPLANATIONS

When I learned that an airplane flying low
over a silver fox farm caused some vixens
to eat their young, I found myself nodding
dumbly, thinking yes, mother stuff, protective,
like that woman who saved her children
from Satan by drowning them in the tub.
Reminded me also of an article I'd read
about a deaf turkey hen who pecked to death
her chicks. Turkey hens, it said,
can only recognize progeny by their cries.

I thought: how unlucky we humans are,
doomed to know what we've done. But no,

the woman who kept her child in a closet
just wanted him to be a good boy, she said,
quiet among her shirts and shoes.
And a man I know—after his wife said hello—
tore their entire house apart. Wouldn't
apologize, didn't know why he should.
Pressures of the job, he explained, deaf
in a way, unreachable, like serial killer
John Wayne Gacy who couldn't hear himself

when he said, "Why would I want to kill those boys, anyway? I'm not their father."

FROM THE TOWER AT THE TOP
OF THE WINDING STAIRS

It seemed that the mountains of Vermont were hunchbacks
ringing their own silent bells, and above them
an opaque, cloudless sky a model of how to remain calm
while other parts of you might be thunder and rain.
From the tower it didn't take long to see the dangers
in believing that seeing was knowing—high-flying birds
revealing our need for angels, some wispy scud
evidence of a past I'd yet to resolve. Still, wasn't
the psychological real? The tower itself had no opinion.
Men and women could be seen planting tomatoes
and rows of lettuce, touching each other good-bye,
and from this height others could be imagined creating
something wonderful out of motives like envy, even spite,
warding off, as they felt it, melancholy's encroachment.
To ascend the tower was to want not to come down.
There to the south—because I had begun to dream—
I could see congressmen suddenly released
from the prisons of their partisanship, wrestling amiably
with the imperfections of human existence. And, beyond,
enemies dropping their guns, asking for forgiveness.
Everything felt comic, how else could it be bearable?
The tower itself was proof I couldn't escape
when I escaped from the world. Out of its side window

I could see a house on fire, and in the distance
cows and goats dotting the hillside, and dogs everywhere—
no matter their size, either forlorn or frisky,
entirely dependent on the goodwill of others.
Soon the night birds would be calling other night birds,
the normal influx of eros begin to mix with music
heard from below. I'd feel it was time to come down,
to touch and be touched, take part in a dailiness
for which I'd need words like welter or maelstrom.
But for now if I looked hard I could see the random
pine cone, the random leaf, and if I closed my eyes
something like a pattern, the semblance of an order.

NOTES

In "Summer Nocturne" the phrase "the space across / which desire reaches" is borrowed from Anne Carson's *Eros the Bittersweet*.